YO-ACG-088

GET THE JOB
YOU
REALLY
WANT-FAST

Alan Jacobson

J. FLORES
PUBLICATIONS
P.O. BOX 830131
MIAMI, FL 33283-0131

**HOW YOU CAN GET THE JOB YOU
REALLY WANT–FAST** by Alan Jacobson

Published by:
J. Flores Publications
P.O. Box 830131
Miami, FL 33283-0131

Direct inquires and/or order to the above address.

ISBN 0-918751-30-6

Library of Congress Catalog Card Number: 94-70388

Printed in the United States of America

This book is dedicated to my wife, Sharon, who has lived through this incredible learning experience with me.

TABLE OF CONTENTS

Introduction

I wonder how many books have been written about finding a job. The number must be immense. But I also wonder how many of those works deal with the realities and core issues of what it takes to find a new job in today's world. Some books are so theoretical that there is very little practical value for the reader. Others deal with a specific topic, such as the psychological issues of the job search. Still others are so specific that they may apply to only one job title or one industry. I say this not to criticize other authors, but to challenge myself to write a more meaningful job search book.

My fervent hope in writing this is that it contains a fair amount of information which will benefit the majority of readers who are engaged in finding new employment. This writing is applicable whether you are currently employed or not. The purpose of this writing is, in reality, to challenge the reader as much as to enlighten him/her. A secondary purpose is to help enlighten hiring managers, and others involved in the employer end of the need to fill jobs, find ways that they can "smooth the flow" with job candidates.

I have asked myself what makes me so qualified to impart critical knowledge on this topic to others who are seeking a job. After all, your choice of employment may be one of the most important decisions you make in your life. The answer to the question has two parts: First, do I have the knowledge, first-hand or otherwise, on the subject? The answer is definitely yes! Having made four successful job searches in five years gives me a great deal of experience. I'm not only a veteran, I'm a pro. I have been to the mountain top. I've been forced to hone my job search skills to a technical science as well as an art form.

Every time I've embarked upon a search, stomach in knots, living on Tums, I've been a little better prepared due to my experience the last time. Yes, I've learned from my mistakes, I have read books, I've received advice— both the requested and welcome kind and the unrequested and not so welcome kind—and I have learned to use this vast pool of knowledge and information to my benefit. Note: It becomes important here to make the distinction between knowledge and information. Information may be neither accurate nor valuable, but knowledge is always both. My intention here is to share knowledge as well as information, but let's focus on the former.

Additionally, having been a hiring manager in many situations qualifies me to understand the employer's perspective. I have been the focal point of dozens of hiring decisions over the years, involving hundreds of candidates and several different firms. And every company has its unique version of the hiring process. Consequently, this book may be of tremendous value to employers to assist them in understanding job candidates and to provide them with a framework for improving their handling of these candidates.

The second part of the answer to the question regarding my qualification to write this book is whether I can take my considerable knowledge on the subject and communicate it in a meaningful way. Can I express myself to you in a way that helps you when you read this book? If you read this book and follow my recommendations, will your job search be more successful or shorter? As an experienced marketing manager, a key part of my career has been spent communicating, writing, conveying messages to a target audience in a meaningful and straightforward way. As an individual who has made a living on written communication, and as a fairly avid (is that a contradiction in terms?) reader, let's hope I have that qualification.

My personal work experience is in the health care field, specifically in the medical device industry. There is no doubt that much of what I write is more specific to that industry than it is generic to all industries. Yet, I can't help but feel that all industries have their little nuances and idiosyncrasies and that a great deal of what I discuss in this book can be directly applied to many different industries and divergent business settings.

Fifteen years medical device experience is a great deal. Nine years with two large corporations and six years with three smaller corporations has given me a broad and deep education. Fifteen years ago, I was a sales rep. Since then, I have had several promotions resulting in my serving in numerous Sales Management and Marketing Management capacities, leading to a Vice President level job. The question that arises here is whether my writing applies to financial people, or to engineers, or to human resources specialists, or manufacturing managers, or the countless other functional areas of business. The answer in each case is a resounding "you bet".

One question that you may want to ask is how successful my job searches could have been since I have had to do four of them in five years. Good question! You may want to first consider the reasons for each search, then ask the question again. I made my first search due to a desire to move upward. There may have been opportunities to stay with my employer at the time and be promoted, but the company headquarters was g.u. (geographically undesirable). The company was located in a town that a friend of mine likes to call Siberacuse due to its isolated location and long, cold winters.

The second search resulted from my company being an acquisition victim. The former parent company lacked an understanding of our core business and chose to divest my company in favor of businesses where they had greater familiarity. The acquiring company did not keep any of our employees.

The third search resulted from what now appears to be a poor job acceptance decision on my part. I had accepted a position with a company run by an entrepreneur. The entrepreneur was a genius at the technical side of his business, but he would rate about a 2 on a scale of 1-10 in business smarts. He simply wouldn't allow us to succeed unless it benefitted his oversized ego. The current business literature is full of cases exactly like this.

My fourth search resulted from taking a risky opportunity with a start-up firm that never succeeded in raising the needed venture capital. I left when the company, unable to meet its financial obligations, owed me almost $85,000 in unpaid compensation. That doesn't included my vested stock in the firm, which is probably worthless even though the principals feel it is extremely valuable.

Today's business environment is dominated by uncertainty. A job can be lost due to management changes, acquisitions, mergers, restructuring, weak sales, business failures, or the disappearance of entire industries. Since very few business people are really secure in their jobs, this book will deal with the knowledge needed to find a new job, the right job, quickly. It won't be easy, but the pain can be reduced and the search can be made easier and shorter in duration.

Oh, No! What Am I Going To Do?

This is usually the first question that pops into everyone's head when they suddenly find that they have lost their job. Horror of horrors! Probably almost everyone faced with the prospect of having to find a job has felt like the man standing on the street corner holding up a sign that says, WILL WORK FOR FOOD. It happens even when there is an *expected* job loss. It's like a bright red neon light flashing in your face, so bright that you can't make it go away even when you close your eyes real tight to block it out. What am I going to do? The obvious answer to this question is you're going to panic.

Go ahead. Let out a scream, tear out your hair. Don't be afraid, this is all normal. Everyone has the right to do this when they suddenly become unemployed. After all, someone has made a conscious decision which resulted in eliminating your means of earning a living, of supporting your lifestyle. They didn't do it with such a negative personal reason in mind, but that is the by-product of a *business decision*. Yes, a business decision, not a personal vendetta against you the individual. Still, it hurts and it is cause for fear and panic. It is a blow to your ego, your sense of self-worth. And more!

12

Now that you know you're normal, what ARE you going to do? In today's unsettled business climate, it is not unusual for individuals to lose their jobs, regardless of their job level, performance, or experience. Sometimes, it just seems as if there isn't any real job security any more. There must be a thousand good reasons why your employment might be terminated. It probably doesn't make you feel any better at first to know that, but prospective employers are aware of the business environment and, consequently, being unemployed shouldn't make you feel stigmatized when you begin to look for a new position.

Beyond that, the current literature supports the idea that job change may be a necessity if you want to move ahead, because career paths are no longer clear cut. The old wisdom that too many job changes will hurt your chances is simply outdated. It has been written recently that the average American will have eight jobs in his/her career. In Europe today, it is not unusual to have four or five jobs on your resume, as compared to two or three just a couple of decades ago. Even in Japan, it is becoming commonplace and acceptable to have more than one employer in your lifetime. *Conventional wisdoms change.* Many progressive companies will not seriously consider a candidate who has spent more than five or six years with his/her present employer. It is perceived to show lack of adaptability.

So, go ahead. Let out that scream. Anger! Outrage! Express your feelings. But sooner or later you have to get in touch with those feelings and get in control of them after you have expressed your anger. A word of caution— don't intentionally or inadvertently allow your family and friends to become the victims of you expressing your emotions. That could become destructive and we are talking about constructive expression here.

There could be a hundred ways to go about looking for a job, and most of them work in the right set of circumstances. In fact, when you find a new position, you will feel that your approach to the search was the correct one. After all, you did find a new job, didn't you? But here we will take the approach that a systematic, carefully planned search will minimize the duration of your unemployment, while maximizing the likelihood that the job you find is the best one for you—both in terms of job satisfaction and compensation. Consider the importance of this when many "authorities" on the subject say it takes an average of one month to find a job for every ten thousand dollars you expect in annual earnings.

Once again, ask yourself "what am I going to do?" You've just had the shock of losing your job, your source of income, the means of supporting your lifestyle and your dreams for the future. If you took my advice, you let out a scream. You panicked, you felt the fears and frustrations of impending doom. Or at least grave uncertainty. Having done this, it is important at this time to develop a tremendous amount of structure in your life and to follow a few important rules.

Rule #1. Allow yourself to *feel* those emotions arising from the job loss.

It is important not to suppress those feelings. Release them. Do not rush head-first, eyes closed into a blind drive to find the first job that comes along, regardless of whether or not it is appropriate for you. Experience the emotions, both over the job loss and the attendant loss of income, and the anxiety over the need to find a new job. Remember—there is a job out there for you. In fact, there are probably several good jobs out there with your name on them. The challenge is to find at least one of them.

Starting Your Search

Your job search needs to be carefully planned. Repeat: Your job search needs to be *carefully* planned. Regardless of whether you are a million dollar a year executive or an entry level employee with one year of experience, an unplanned, haphazard approach to finding a job is not in your best interest. You will not harm yourself by waiting a day or two after you lose your job to begin the search. On the contrary, by taking off a day or two you can clear your mind while dealing with the emotional pain of losing your last job. Then, and only then, is it the time to begin planning your job search.

Rule #2. Carefully plan your job search in order to minimize your period of unemployment and to ultimately find the best job for you.

Carefully planning your job search not only will make you more productive in finding a new position, it will discipline your mind. That kind of mental discipline is critical to the job-seeker for several reasons. The first of these is that it keeps you focused.

Rule #3. Commit to yourself that the job search is a full time job in itself and that it is the most important single activity in your life right now.

The second reason that mental discipline is critical is that you must force yourself to spend forty to sixty hours per week looking for your new job. Anything less represents lack of commitment. Lack of commitment will prevent you from sticking to the task. And you need to stick to the task in order to be successful.

Acknowledge to yourself that you will spend eight, ten, or twelve hours per day in your job search. Sometimes, the search can be boring. Other times it can be

tedious,

burdensome,

taxing,

frustrating,

frightening,

disappointing,

exhausting,

discouraging,

horrifying,

and many other negative adjectives. (The section of this book dealing with attitude will further elucidate this topic.)

Sometimes, believe it or not, your search can be

challenging,

stimulating,

educational,

uplifting,

enlightening,

exciting,
interesting,
fascinating,
or many other positive things to you. Unfortunately, this is the case only a small percentage of the time. As they say in the boy scouts, be prepared.

The core reason for being disciplined is so that you can project an organized picture of yourself to your prospective employers. Keep your mind agile, don't become a worrier or, worse yet, don't become immobilized by fear. You can keep your mind agile by reading or engaging in any activities that require mental involvement.

Rule #4. Only you can make it happen. Employers are not likely to seek you out. You will find a job for only one reason—because you made it happen.

The Set-Up

What do you need to organize your job search? You will need several tools, many of which you may already have. Of course a lot of this seems elementary. You probably don't need some author to tell you what you need, but it is important to have all the right tools:

Office
Desk
Telephone
Answering Device
Computer
Envelopes and Postage
Office supplies

Rule #5. Having all the right tools will allow you to be more efficient and make your search easier to handle.

Office. The first thing you need is a place where you can work. An office, a den, a corner of another room will do. But it must be conducive to work. If there is a television or a stereo in the room, don't turn them on. *No distractions,* please. This is going to require a great deal of concentration. And quiet. And proper lighting.

The office becomes the physical environment of your search. You will spend a great deal of time here until you accept a job offer. The right physical environment is critical to your success.

Desk. The room should have a desk, or at least a table where you can spread out your papers, directories, work materials, etc. Ideally, the desk or table should be used only for your job search. If you have children, and you can arrange it, it is best if they do their homework elsewhere.

Telephone And Answering Device. The next step is to have adequate support materials on your desk. The most important tool in your job search is your telephone. You must be able to call prospective employers as well as receive return calls from them. Just about everyone in America has at least one telephone today. Modern telephone software options, such as call waiting, will make your telephone more versatile.

You should also have an automated answering device, for the obvious reasons. You definitely want to get your phone messages, even when you are out on an interview or doing research. In spite of being impersonal, it is much more professional to have your phone answered by an answering device than for your children, spouse, roommate, etc, to take your messages. Or worse yet, you don't want to be in the situation where you are unavailable and cannot receive messages at all. You may appreciate the need for your answering device if you consider it to be a low tech form of "voice mail."

Computer. Next in importance among your job search tools, after the telep! ne and answering device, is the personal computer. Statistics indicate that many families have a PC in the home today. With good word processing software, you can accomplish all of your organizing tasks and record keeping with a minimum of work.

And good spreadsheet software will allow you to keep excellent track of your expenses for tax purposes. It is important to remember that much of what you spend in your job search will be tax deductible next year. Keep good accurate records and let your accountant or tax preparer help you determine what is deductible on Federal and state income taxes. This may include telephone charges, postage, office supplies, the cost of sending fax messages, copies, mileage in your car, travel and entertainment, and many other expenses.

One excellent way to keep track of all the companies you contact and the status of each one is to keep an alphabetical listing on the computer. This will allow you to readily access each one, including phone numbers, contact names, chronological contact history, follow-up dates, and so on.

As you begin each day, you will be able to scan the alphabetical listing to determine your action list for that day. Visually scanning a list to determine today's activities, even a list of two to three hundred company names, will require only a few minutes. Below each company name you should keep a complete record of names and dates of all phone calls and correspondence, expected dates of next communication, notes about conversations, and any other information that you may need to reference. Don't waste your energy by attempting to memorize anything.

Another benefit of good word processing software is that you will be able to minimize the time you spend writing letters. Take some time to carefully write just a few letters—an introductory (cold call) letter, an "I was referred to you by... letter, a follow-up to a phone call letter, and a follow-up to an interview letter, for example. Keep these letters in memory (hard drive or floppy), then simply personalize each one and print it without having to reinvent the wheel every time you need to send correspondence. You will save huge amounts of time and still have correspondence that looks and reads "professional."

You may want to do the same thing with your resume. It can be extremely advantageous to have several resumes, each one highlighting different facets of your experience and ability. An example of this is if you have experience in two functional areas and want to apply for positions in both. If you have experience in both sales and marketing, you may have a resume that focuses on your sales accomplishments and one that focuses on your marketing accomplishments. Simply recall from memory the one you want, personalize it as needed for the individual you are sending it to, and print it. A good printer with your PC will give you letter quality resumes and correspondence.

A chronological correspondence file seems to be the best way to catalogue your written communications. Simply file a copy of each letter in the front of the file as you go, and you will have it all filed neatly in reverse chronological order. Cross-referencing letters with the alphabetical listing on the computer will provide you with a quick and simple way to file and relocate any letters you may have sent.

Do make sure that your PC is in tip-top working order. It becomes your second most valuable tool, after the telephone. Keep an adequate supply of paper and an extra ribbon or ink source.

Postage, Envelopes, And Office Supplies. Needless to say, you need envelopes and postage in order to send your correspondence and resume to prospective employers. It is important to send your resume to the proper individuals as soon as possible after they ask for it. Usually, this means employing the U.S. mail.

Occasionally, in urgent situations, it might mean using Federal Express or sending a fax. Federal Express is the most expensive (about $15), but the most effective and controllable means of getting your resume to a hiring official overnight. A fax, if you don't own a fax machine, may cost about $5 for a two page resume and a cover letter. If you don't have a fax machine in your home (and most of us do not), there are a couple of means of getting access to one. If you can afford one, by all means purchase it. In the absence of your own fax machine, the ideal situation is one where a business person you know allows you access to his or her machine at no charge or for a small fee.

The more realistic means, however, is through a business that provides fax service to the public on a fee basis. Since this can add up to a significant expense at a time when you don't have much income, always qualify the urgency of your prospect seeing your resume today. Use the mail if it is not urgent.

The Self-Evaluation

Okay. So you lost your job, you lost your cool, you regained your composure, and you set up your office to begin your job search. Before you can begin looking for a new job, there are some evaluative questions that must be answered.

What am I looking for?

And the corollaries to that include, what have I done prior to now in my career?

What am I capable of doing?

What are my strengths and what are my weaknesses?

What components of my experience and abilities will an employer find useful or valuable?

How can I improve my value?

Are there any aspects of my background that will provide an obstacle to being hired?

How much do I realistically expect to earn?

What are my most important accomplishments?

What is my level of commitment to the type of job I am seeking?

Am I mentally prepared for the job search process?

How good am I at what I do compared to other potential candidates?

Can I make a difference with my performance and have I made a difference in the past?

The self-evaluation involves thoughtfully and honestly answering these and other questions, plus writing a resume. Or, more specifically, as we mentioned earlier, writing several resumes. For example, if your background includes Marketing, Sales, and Business Development, you may have three resumes—one to focus on your accomplishments in each of these areas. Don't be confused into thinking that any of these resumes misrepresent the truth! On the contrary, each one will highlight that portion of your accomplishments that you want to call to the attention of a specific employer.

Rule #6. How you see yourself and how you project your self image plays a significant role in determining how employers react to you in making hiring decisions.

First, however, we must continue with self-evaluation. How would you define yourself, careerwise, in one or two sentences? Prospective employers may ask you to do that. It is not uncommon for a hiring manager to ask, "What is it that you are looking for?" You must be fully prepared to answer the question. You may, for example, consider yourself to be a career Marketing Manager with specific strength in Sales. Or you may be a financially oriented general manager with intensive business development experience. Or you may be a financial officer with emphasis on venture capital. The possibilities are endless. But you must be able to define your career accomplishments and goals to your own satisfaction before you can concisely explain your goals and abilities to a hiring manager.

It helps if your experience and your goals are related. If not, this may represent a career change. While it is considered acceptable to change careers once, or even twice in some cases, you may want to get professional employment counseling before embarking upon a career change.

The career change situation may be beyond the scope of this book.

Once you have answered the key questions to your own satisfaction, it is time to begin writing those resumes. And it is time to *begin making decisions* about where you want to work.

Identifying Companies You Want To Work For

How do I choose thee? Let me count the ways. There are numerous criteria that can be used to choose potential employers or to eliminate them from consideration. For example, you may choose to contact companies based upon any of the following:

Location
Industry
Size
Structure
Reputation
Stage in Life Cycle
Commitment to R&D
Growth Rate
Management Style

Just to name a few. The key element here is that *you may choose*! Many hiring managers consider themselves to be in complete control of the hiring process. Not true! Hiring managers have a great deal of control over who they hire. But you, as a candidate, will make the final decision. It takes two to tango, and all the other cliches. In reality, you

are likely to be rejected more times than you make the final
negative decision, yet the process is incomplete until you,
the candidate, make the affirmative decision to accept an
employer's offer. More important, though, by determining the characteristics of the company you want to work
for and the job you want, you will be consciously eliminating many potential employers at the beginning of your
search and as you move through the process.

Rule #7. Being selective in choosing companies to contact
is a sign that you are exercising control.

Selecting prospective employers can be a difficult and
arduous task, but it is a critical one. Furthermore, it is the
first step that puts you in control of the process.

The first question you may want to answer for yourself
is, "Where, geographically, do I want to work?" You must
determine your willingness to relocate. Do you want to
stay put or are you willing to move to another city? If you
are willing to relocate, are there geographical limitations
to where you will go? For example, you may have a first
preference for remaining in your present town. But you
may be willing to consider locations in your region or
specific other areas of the country. You may not even have
a geographical preference.

Write down your preference.

Your second selection criterion may be the specific industry or industries you are willing or qualified to work
in. For example, taking a subject near and dear to my
heart, you may have experience in, and the desire to
remain in, the medical device industry. On the other hand,
your ability may be purely functional (such as accounting

or financial) and not industry dependent. Write down your preference and your abilities.

The next means of classifying potential employers is by size. You may prefer only large companies because of the security. Or you might prefer small companies because of the rapid growth and greater potential for personal advancement. Write it down.

These are all characteristics of firms that can be readily identified, or quantified, externally. Some of the other evaluative criteria may not be so readily discernable. You may have to do in-depth research or even interview with a company to find out about its commitment to R&D, its structure, its growth rate, or its management style and culture. That's okay. By learning what is easy to identify, you will be much more focused in your search.

Once you have completed these steps, you can begin compiling a preliminary list of potential employers. The key word is preliminary, because your list will continue to grow and expand as long as your search lasts. You can get this information from numerous sources, but assume that you are going to become far more familiar with the facilities of your public library or a nearby business school. Your librarian will be able to assist you in finding industrial guides that have information about companies on a geographical basis. To the best of my knowledge, most states have published industrial guides listing firms by SIC (standard industrial classification).

In the medical device industry, the *Medical Device Register* is the ultimate source of company information. You should use guides such as these to generate a list of the firms in the areas where you want to work, in the industries that are important to you. An initial listing may be several firms, or several hundred firms. One critical fact to remember is that you will be forced to broaden your search over time, so your list will continue to grow. The offshoot of this is that you do not need a comprehensive list to begin—only a good list.

For each firm on your list, get an address, phone number, and contact names if possible. Keep in mind that many firms today have toll free or "800" numbers. (These may or may not be easy to find. My experience is that 800 directory assistance doesn't even have most of them.) You don't have to be a rocket scientist to recognize that you can save hundreds of dollars every month if you don't have to pay for the calls. Don't be self-conscious, the first time you call, about asking the receptionist if there is a toll free number. Only a fool throws away money. And remember, this is a time when your expenses are immense, but your income may be zero or merely an unemployment check.

As you prepare to begin contacting the companies on your list, prepare a written outline of what you want to say to each person you call. Don't wing it. No matter how good you are at improvisational conversation, you should avoid the risk of not knowing what to say next. Be prepared and sound prepared. And strive toward your goal when you make each call.

Rule #8. Every phone call should be made with a specific objective in mind.

Even though your ultimate objective is to receive an acceptable job offer, there are intermediate goals. It may require numerous phone calls and two or three interviews before you get to the offer stage. And if you are in control, remember, you may choose to eliminate some companies along the way.

Regarding call objectives, for example, you will want to learn the names of the key contacts, their secretaries, whether they have any suitable job openings, have someone agree to review your resume, schedule a telephone interview or personal interview, etc. Put all the company names on your alphabetical computer listing, along with phone numbers, contact names, contact dates, follow-up information, and any other information you might need to recall.

Don't rely on your memory. Eliminate mind clutter by recording everything. Do you know what mind clutter is? It is potentially useful information floating around in your head which may attract your attention at an inopportune moment. Have you ever been almost asleep at night when you suddenly remember something you need to do tomorrow? Then you have to disturb your sleep to get up and make a written note in order to avoid forgetting. Or you may be watching a movie when you suddenly remember something you forgot to do. You should eliminate this kind of mind clutter.

Actually Doing The Search

The active search itself is quite a simple affair. It requires:
diligence,
commitment,
tenacity,
determination,
perseverance,
self respect,
hard work,
and much much more.

What I would consider the best way to conduct your job search in the real world is to commit eight to ten hours a day and stick to it. Wake up early, get ready to work, and begin calling employers from your list. Make a daily list of who you want or need to contact that day and begin calling. Be sure to take time zones into consideration if your search involves varied regions of the country. Use the time zones to your advantage by calling earlier in the day, later in the day, and other regions when your time zone is at lunch.

There will be times when you want to give up and stop

calling. Ignore the temptation and keep at it. Eventually, you may arrive at a time when you have nothing left to do and the day is not over. If you absolutely positively irrevocably cannot move forward, and you've been working at this for a while, take off part of the day and do something different as a diversion. Just don't allow yourself this luxury too often.

Cold calls

My personal preference in cold call situations is to contact the highest ranking officer whose name I can find in each company. For some strange reasons, it is usually easier to reach the president of a company than someone two or three levels lower in the organization. The president usually came to be president because of the ability to manage time effectively, among other things. The result is that I have often been able to reach the president of a company on the first call, or he/she may even return my call the same day when the only message I left is my name and phone number. A manager at a lower level would have greater difficulty balancing the schedule to find time to speak with me. Lower level managers are also more likely to be impressed with their own importance. "I don't know that person. Why should I return the call?"

Rule #9. Always make your initial contact, in a cold call situation, at the top of the organization or the highest level that may be appropriate.

There is another advantage of speaking with the president. That occurs when he/she refers you to another manager within the company. You should always ask the president if you can use his/her name when you speak to the other manager. They typically say yes, and mentioning the president nearly always opens the door with subordinate managers. "Mr. Jones, I was referred to you by Ms. Elaine Blackstone, your president, in regard to a specific (or potential) job opportunity."

Depending upon the level of job you are seeking, however, it may not be appropriate to speak with the president of the company. Start at the highest level you can. If not the president, you should probably contact the vice president of the functional area where you want to work. The VP of Finance, Marketing, Sales, Engineering, etc. will be aware of openings within his/her department and can refer you, if necessary, to the specific hiring manager who is directly responsible. Once again, ask to use the VP's name because it will definitely get the attention of the manager who reports to him/her.

Secretaries

When calling a business manager's office, you will most likely speak with a secretary first. The secretary is someone who the president or vice president trusts implicitly. That secretary can play an enormous role in the level of success you will ultimately achieve in making contact in that company. Depending upon how you interact, she (usually they are women) can be your best friend or your worst enemy within that company. It is imperative that you make the secretary your ally or she will become a major obstacle. The choice is yours.

How, you may ask? Start by introducing yourself and asking her name. Record her name in your computer files. Be specific in telling her why you are calling and, in a warm personable manner, ask for her help. Tell her that you are calling her boss because you are looking for a job, that you have some relevant experience, and ask to speak to him/her. She may elect to connect you immediately, but most of the time the boss won't be available when you call.

The secretary has the ability to see that the boss returns your call or refers you to another manager within the firm. Depending upon the way she presents your message to her boss, she can also encourage him/her to ignore you. You know the implied tone in "this person called you again looking for a job." As opposed to "this gentleman/lady called in regard to a position with this company. He/she has a great deal of experience and sounded quite professional on the telephone." It's obvious which one will benefit you most.

If the boss does refer you to a subordinate, ask the secretary if you can use his/her name and tell the manager you were referred to him/her by the president's office (use the president's name).

You should know the secretary's name on all follow up calls you make to that office. Always identify yourself and speak in a friendly manner with her. The other side of the coin is a nightmare. If you are belligerent to her, the secretary will help you find the back door.

Human Resources Departments

In order to know what to expect from your contact with a company's human resources department, you need to understand the role of HR in the recruiting and hiring process. It varies significantly from one company to another. Ask someone from another department what role

Human Resources plays in the process. A section on HR departments follows later in this book.

How Companies Recruit And Hire

Recruiting

Recruiting and hiring are two related but distinct activities, usually separated/connected by the selection process. Recruiting is fairly straightforward. It is the function of identifying and locating individuals who may have the necessary qualifications to perform well in a given job.

Regardless of the size of a company, the recruiting process begins with the recognized need for an individual to fill a position. That position may have become vacant due to another individual leaving a job or it may be a newly created position due to growth. The larger and more structured the organization, the more likely a formal process exists where the recognized need becomes a written request requiring a series of approvals. Eventually, the result is a written job description including a summary of job skills and experience that the ideal candidate will possess.

The operative word here is "ideal." Many hiring managers will leave critical jobs unfilled for long periods of time, even months, because of an unexplainable belief that they must find the ideal candidate, not merely a highly qualified individual with an outstanding record of accomplishment. Further explanation is ahead under *hiring* and *the ideal candidate.*

As you move along in the search, you may find a number of situations where you feel that you are a near perfect match for the job requirements, only to find yourself rejected due to the lack of some minute tidbit of job experience. Don't take this personally. Instead, be prepared to sell yourself as the "near perfect candidate, lacking only one minor detail," and be prepared to explain how you can more than compensate for the shortcoming by taking advantage of your strengths.

You may in fact be nearly ideal versus the requirements for a job, but the hiring manager may have written hiring specs based upon his/her own credentials or that of the individual who was just promoted upward from that job. File this occurrence under unrealistic expectations, and hope that it only occurs when you come across inexperienced hiring authorities. Remember that the employer is in control at this stage of the process. Your objective is to get an offer, then you will be in control of the choices. As Andy Rooney might say, "Did you ever wonder why the job requires ten years of experience?" Wouldn't six or eight years be sufficient if everything else fits?

Rule #10. Keep your cool, be convincing, and don't let the quirks of a hiring manager undermine your attitude.

One unfortunate side effect of today's economy is that there are often more candidates than jobs and, consequently, employers may be successful in approximating that ideal candidate. It used to be that a candidate with eight out of ten qualifications would get the job, but today it often seems to take ten out of ten. In order to avoid being victimized by this, you need to make a compelling case for the qualifications that you do have. "Sell" yourself to the hiring manager.

A key component of the recruitment process, particularly in larger companies, is the role of the Human Resources Department in the process. Many of these people are not familiar with the real-world implications of the written job requirements, and therefore may make recommendations based upon their limited perceptions. Human Resources managers may inadvertently eliminate outstanding candidates whose abilities differ from the written specs. This can happen to you. But, because HR people may do some of the preliminary screening, and because they may be intimately familiar with the personalities involved, they are critical to the process. It is part of their job to perform some of the recruiting and hiring functions.

Most often, the first step to fill a job vacancy is for a company to look internally for qualified candidates who are already employed by the firm in other capacities. This is often an outstanding means of locating qualified individuals, and promotions have a positive impact on company morale. Furthermore, it reduces risk because the candidates and the company know each other equally well. So job openings may be "posted" on a bulletin board for everyone to see.

When the search for internal candidates fails, hiring managers seek qualified individuals outside the firm. Typically, the eyes of the search look to competitors or to other firms within the industry. In many cases, the firm will seek referrals from other employees and other outside sources to identify a pool of potential talent to begin the selection and hiring process.

Selection

A hiring manager will always prefer to have a number of qualified candidates arise in the recruitment process in order to make the selection process more competitive. Every manager's preference is different, but most will prefer to select from a fairly large pool of talented recruits. My personal preference as a hiring manager is to begin the selection process by having brief telephone interviews with about a dozen of the candidates whose resumes best fit my hiring criteria. I will then select the best four or five for personal interviews.

Resumes are really pot luck, no matter what you may have heard or read. Everyone reads resumes differently, looking for different writing styles, different job histories, educational backgrounds, etc. There is no one best way to structure your resume so that everyone will read it to your maximum benefit. One rule that seems to apply, though, is the two page maximum. For anything longer than that, it may really benefit you most to have several resumes highlighting different facets of your abilities and accomplishments. Several types of formats may be effective, but you should always highlight your accomplishments. A sample of one resume format that seems to work is included in the appendix to this book. Also in the appendix is a brief list of what not to include in your resume.

As a hiring manager, what I usually do in the resume stage is look for two or three broad impact criteria for screening purposes. Criteria such as technical knowledge, critical skills, or specific customer involvement. Beyond that, I may zero in on one or two more skills in the phone interview process, such as communication skills, in order to narrow down the field. I don't like to interview more than five or six candidates for a position and, on the other side of the coin, it typically doesn't please me to know that I am in a large field of candidates when I am interviewing for a job.

I recently declined an interview for an apparently good position due to the fact that there were eighteen candidates. How confusing! In a group larger than six or eight candidates, it seems that it has to be perplexing for the interviewer to remember each candidate and his or her strengths. Imagine yourself, a hiring manager, over a two or three day period, interviewing twenty candidates for a job. Could you remember many of them? Of course not!. You will most likely remember the first and last of the candidates and those that stand out for physical reasons. It is unfair to himself/herself for a manager to presume that he/she can do much better. Therefore it may be in your best interest to know the size of the field before the interview.

A well-prepared interviewer will ask most of the same questions of each candidate in order to get a fair comparison. That manager will then choose the best candidates to move on to the next step in the process. So it is critical to provide strong, concise answers to the questions. (More later in the interview section.)

It is important to understand this process in order to function well in the environment.

Hiring
A hiring decision will typically be the final step in the

recruitment process. In most searches, the final candidates will all be nearly equal in qualifications and accomplishments. The final decision, however, will be made most of the time on the basis of interpersonal chemistry. The manager will hire the individual who he/she feels most comfortable with on a personal basis. Without regard to the actual fairness, it is reality. Be prepared.

The final hiring decision can potentially be made by a number of people, either individually or as a committee. The final choice is often the most qualified individual for the job, and equally often is not. Interesting, but mostly subjective means are used in reality in making the choice. Most managers will overlook objective means of evaluation (qualifications) in favor of intangibles such as looks—not to be confused with appearance—where you went to school, and other non-specific value judgments.

Allow me to expand upon this a little bit. We all enjoy being surrounded by attractive people. In a close contest, most managers will select the most handsome candidate. It may also be to your advantage if you are a 6′3″ male as opposed to 5′8″. Or in the case of women, if you are 5′8″ instead of 5′1″. Also, most managers will favor a candidate they consider "interesting" over one they consider ultimately qualified, but dull. An athletic candidate will be preferred over a less physical individual. But most important of all, the key intangible is enthusiasm. Enthusiasm is contagious. If you are enthusiastic about yourself, your background, and the interview, the hiring managers are more likely to be enthusiastic about you.

Remember, the hiring manager will make the final decision based on factors other than qualifications. Qualifications only get you past the first round.

Networking

Finding job leads is one of the important steps in ultimately being hired for a position. The next chapter will include a detailed discussion of the many ways to develop a repertoire of job leads. But first, we need to discuss NETWORKING. What is networking? Everyone talks about it. Do you really understand how to use networking to the maximum benefit in your job search?

Networking is nothing more than the sharing with your peers of information about the status of the job market. Networking is talking with individuals or groups of people to learn quickly what they may have had to learn through weeks or months of effort. And, the flip side is sharing what you have learned through your own weeks and months of effort.

Rule #11. Networking is, by far, the most valuable means of finding job leads.

There are two basic ways to network. The first is through personal contacts, and the second is via networking groups or organizations.

Networking via personal contacts

Begin by making a list of everyone you know in your

business and your field. Include past employers and supervisors, peers, competitors, and everyone else you
know. Call each of these people. Be frank and tell them
what your goals are. (Remember that you defined your
goals when you began your search.) Ask each individual
probing questions about opportunities they may be aware
of. Ask about openings they may have applied for, openings they may have heard about, or openings within their
firm or in competing firms. The key is to ask the right
questions. Plan your questions, and write them down,
before you begin making your calls.

Of course, some of these people won't give you the time
of day. You should expect that. But some of them will give
you exactly what you want. You will call some of these
people only once, but a few will want to become part of
your search and you will have regular conversations to
discuss new openings they may have become aware of.

I recall a particular manager at a well known multi-bil-
lion dollar company who I was somehow put in contact
with via the telephone. He gave me several tips, one
resulting in an interview, and we maintained telephone
contact for a couple of months. Then, I had the good
fortune to meet him at a Cardiology conference in Atlanta.
We strengthened our relationship and maintained contact
for a couple of years. I still call him periodically and he
even calls me on occasion to see how I'm doing. He has
given me immeasurable volumes of valuable information
about his company, his competition, and the industry in
general. This is the ultimate kind of networking contact.

Don't be reluctant to call people like this. They don't
have to be your best friends to be valuable networking
contacts. You might be surprised at the opportunities that

you uncover. The best jobs, and the most valuable opportunities, are often uncovered by networking. Reliance on newspaper ads or recruiters will only expose you to a small percentage of the job opportunities out there. And the more opportunities you apply for, the greater the likelihood that you will find a good position quickly.

One key source of networking leads is the employers you contact on a cold call basis. Many people you call or write to will simply tell you that they don't have any appropriate openings at the present time. They often want to end the conversation by asking you to send a resume in the event that a suitable opening occurs. This is sometimes legitimate; other times it is a conversation closer. Before you say goodbye, ask if that manager knows of any openings at other firms for an individual with your background. You may preface your question with a preamble, such as:

"I know you've been in this line of work for a fairly long time and you've been successful. You must have excellent knowledge of what goes on in the industry, as well as strong contacts. Are you aware of any openings at other companies where they might be looking for someone with my experience?"

You'll be amazed at the response you get. Of course, some people will simply say no. Others will give you company names, managers' names, or in some cases even job titles of open positions. These are almost always the best source of job leads. Remember, everyone you speak with becomes a potential networking source.

Often, in your job search, you will meet other job seekers. Do yourself a favor and network with them. True, you may be competing with these people for some positions, but you can help each other without compromising yourself. Of course, you wouldn't want to divulge information about an opening where you are currently in contention for an offer. Neither would anybody else. However, you can tell these people about openings you chose not to pursue, or jobs that do not interest you, or openings where you have been eliminated from consideration for some reason. They will, needless to say, be glad to do the same for you. Everyone's goals and experiences are a little bit different, so what isn't right for another candidate might become a great opportunity for you. Keep a list of names and phone numbers of all your network contacts and maintain communication with them.

Networking groups

There has been an emergence of networking organizations around the country in the last couple of years. These are either informal or structured organizations that meet on a regular basis to foster the exchange of information by job-seekers. One of these groups, for example, meets weekly in the Boston area. The name of the organization is WIND—Wednesday Is Networking Day. Groups such as WIND often meet for breakfast where everyone pays a small fee which covers the cost of breakfast and allows the organizers to make a small profit.

Some of the groups meet in the evening. Some are free, some charge per meeting, and others charge a one time membership fee. These meetings and the groups tend to be well worth the cost. Depending upon the size and level of structure, the groups may have smaller sub-groups by industry or functional specialty where those members exchange what they have learned about the market in the past week. Some of the organizations even have periodic publications, the cost being covered by their membership dues. An incidental benefit of these groups is that members who find jobs will typically become excellent sources for jobs and job information for other members.

In most major metropolitan areas, formal or informal networking groups exist today. Information about them can typically be found in the classified sections of the local newspapers. *The National Business Employment Weekly* is also an excellent source of information about networking group meetings, workshops, and job search support groups from all regions of the U.S.

Remember that networking is an incredibly valuable source of job information. Most good jobs are not advertised in the newspaper and are not recruited via "headhunters."

Addendum to Networking

One excellent place for networking is at trade shows. Exhibitions and trade shows are gathering places for the players in a given industry. If you are aware of a trade show in your industry, and you should make it your business to be aware of them, it is highly recommended that you attend. Key executives from many firms will be there, and it is an excellent opportunity to see a company's products.

Obtain a list of exhibitors and call them to make as many appointments as you can ahead of time. Then, fill in the remaining exhibit hours by visiting as many display booths as possible and meeting the key managers of each firm. If the individual you wish to see is not in attendance, ask for his/her name and use the name of the person you meet in the booth as a referral. (Always ask permission). This will open the door for you to make contact when you return from the show.

Secondarily, many of those people manning the booths will be able to provide you with excellent networking information. These people are your peers and will usually be willing to share any information they may have about job openings at their firm or at others.

The value of trade shows for networking cannot be overstated. In verification of this point, allow me to explain how I networked at a major trade show two years ago. Prior to leaving for the medical show/conference, I requested a list of exhibitors. From the list, I had scheduled nine interviews over three days and evenings (yes, evenings). In total, I ended up seeing the key executives in over thirty companies in those three days, one of whom made me a job offer two weeks after the show. Another one ended up making me a job offer two years later. So it really works.

Sources of Job Leads

There are so many possible sources of job leads, but let's categorize them into the following:

Networking
Classified advertising
Recruiters/Headhunters
Industrial guides

Since we have just concluded a discussion of networking, this chapter will focus on classified advertising, recruiters/headhunters, and other means of identifying companies and jobs. (Networking, in the broadest sense of the term, includes the use of personal contacts and referrals.)

Classified advertising

It has been estimated that 10% to 20% of all jobs appear in classified advertising. That doesn't represent a particularly large segment of the potential jobs for you during your search, but it is nonetheless an avenue that must not be overlooked.

Most of the jobs you find in the classified section of your local newspaper are well-defined positions where the need to fill the jobs has some degree of urgency. One notable exception to this is a few small companies that run ads periodically just to see what kind of talent is available on the market and to determine what the price tag for that talent will be. It is difficult to become aware of who is doing this until you have been confronted with the situation more than once. A particular small medical device company on the Connecticut shore comes to mind. About once every couple of months, they seem to run a classified ad for a position that would be an excellent match for my talents and experience. For about a year and a half I followed up on these ads, but I only chuckle when I see them now. The scenario goes something like this:

I respond in writing to the ad. They call me and ask me to come in for an interview. I go in for an interview replete with a recitation of the description of the entrepreneur as the "benevolent dictator." They then proceed to tell me that the position has not yet been defined or not yet approved. I'm flabbergasted because the ad was very specific. Other people have told me of the same experience with this company. Recognize it if it happens to you.

Newspaper ads tend to be reasonably specific as to what skills and background are required. This is clearly an advantage to the candidate because you know up front how you match the company's expectations. Beware of non-specific ads. These tend to be aimed at individuals who are unsure of themselves or who do not have well-defined goals. A company that is unsure of itself may not be a good potential employer.

One key concept is to not limit yourself to one specific newspaper in your study of the classified section. Of course you want to read the ads in your local newspaper or newspapers. Beyond that, however, are additional sources of job opportunities. The *Wall Street Journal* is an excellent source, particularly their weekly publication, *The National Business Employment Weekly*. This can be purchased at a newsstand, via subscription, or, better yet, can be accessed weekly in the reference room of your local library. The *Weekly* includes a compilation of all the employment ads in all regional editions of the *Wall Street Journal* for the previous week. It also includes some excellent articles relevant to the job search.

The *National Ad Search* is another weekly publication which compiles and classifies by job title employment opportunities from approximately seventy-five major newspapers throughout the country. It gives you access to employment opportunities throughout the United States. The *Ad Search* may be available at your public library.

A few particularly well-known newspapers tend to be vehicles for ads from diverse parts of the country. For example, the *New York Times* is considered a tremendous advertising source by many companies outside the New York area because of the rich talent pool that reads the *Times*. As a result, it is not uncommon to see ads in the *Times* from companies in Michigan, Ohio, North Carolina, and other states. You will be doing yourself a favor if you buy the Sunday *New York Times* for its classified section, or at least read it in the reference room in your local library.

Some companies run blind ads in the classified section of the newspaper, where they describe an available position but do not give the name of the company. Blind ads are often justified by the company if an employee is soon to be fired or if management does not want present employees to know of the search. Still, you may want to avoid these. I have rarely ever received an answer or even an acknowledgement from a blind ad. Even an ad from a company you are not familiar with is far better than an ad without a company name. In the worst case, unscrupulous recruiters will run classified ads for attractive but non-existent jobs in order to attract qualified applicants for their files.

One down-side to answering newspaper ads is that the competition is incredibly fierce. Not that this isn't always the situation with job openings of other origin, but in today's market newspaper ads may attract hundreds of responses. In my own experience, when I have placed ads for sales people or sales managers in a newspaper, I usually get over a hundred responses. Even though I have been specific in the ad regarding job requirements, I end up having to read over a hundred resumes and cover letters, seventy five percent of them belonging to people who don't appear to be even remotely qualified. For example, "I've been a flight attendant for seven years, so I'm sure I can be a sales manager." This is why the vast majority of jobs do not appear in the classified section of your newspaper—most hiring managers want to avoid the aggravation of qualifying a vast pool of applicants.

There *are* a number of good jobs available primarily through classified ads. Do not eliminate them as a source. Many companies would prefer having to screen a massive pile of resumes to using a recruiter. There are advantages to this approach. Recruiters are very costly, and cost conscious companies believe, right or wrong, that in today's economy they can attract the best candidates with a classified ad. They feel that many qualified individuals will read the ad and respond and, therefore, the cost of a recruiter may not be justified.

One of the things about classified ads that really makes me angry is the array of job titles that you see. The best example of this is "Marketing Representative." What in the hell is a Marketing Representative? The answer is simple: it is a euphemistic title, very attractive on the surface, which obscures the reality of the job requirements while attempting to make the job sound more noble in scope. For example, a marketing rep, aside from being an oxymoron, is a sales rep. Period. Good sales reps will respond to an ad for a sales rep. I wonder who responds to an ad for a marketing rep! Dreamers? Marketing is vastly different from sales. A sales rep's job is very different from a marketing manager's job. Why would anyone want to confuse them?

Recruiters/Headhunters

I recommend *Rites of Passage at $100,000*, by John Lucht if you want to gain real insight into how recruiters work. Still, I will include a short description of how to work with headhunters in order to avoid any major gaps in this book.

There are essentially two types of recruiters: Retainer recruiting firms and contingency recruiters, also known as headhunters. Some headhunters hate the moniker, while others proudly refer to themselves as such. There are a few highly successful, highly specialized recruiters who do not fit into either of these categories, but the odds are that you won't be working with any of them.

Retainer recruiting firms operate by conducting searches for companies, while being paid on a retainer basis. In other words, they contract to fill specific jobs for a predetermined fee, and they are paid whether they are successful in finding the right candidate or not. They typically are more structured and seem more professional than headhunters, although this may not always be true.

Retainer recruiting firms have the capability to provide a number of services for their clients, going beyond sending screened resumes to the hiring managers. They often conduct interviews, provide assistance with training and development, help to write job descriptions, and provide assistance in a number of human resource related areas. They do most of the leg work for their clients in the recruitment, selection, and hiring process. From a candidate's point of view, they seem to deliver an accurate appraisal of the company's goals, strengths and weaknesses, as well as profiles of the key managers.

Most retainer firms work on an exclusive basis only, not sharing job openings with other firms. The fees are usually in the range of 30% of the first year earnings of the jobs they fill. Retainer firms will likely refer you to the hiring manager for an interview if they feel that the interpersonal chemistry is right and if you have the vast majority of the necessary qualifications for the job.

Headhunters are a bit different. They typically work for about the same fee as the retainer firm, but they don't always have an exclusive on a given job and they don't get paid unless they fill the position. They are also known as contingency recruiters, the contingency being whether they find the right candidates for the positions. Many of them also don't do much more for a hiring company than provide an initial screening of resumes, conduct brief phone interviews, and forward qualified resumes to the hiring manager. How does it feel to know that you're nothing more than a qualified resume?

Although that sounds like a negatively biased question, I will attempt to provide an unprejudiced description of what headhunters can do. There are a few headhunters with whom I maintain an excellent relationship, but I hope the remainder of them will carefully consider the total package of implications of their actions. I will cite two examples of why it seems as if my bias against recruiters is justified.

First, I think of one particular recruiter who I have known for several years. Over the last eight to ten years, he has placed a few candidates with me. He has also called me regularly to find out if my hiring needs have recently changed. Always cordial and concerned, he made sure to keep in touch with my needs. That was until the time I called him to tell him I was looking for a job and that I could use his help. He asked for an updated resume, told me that he'd get to work on it, and never called back again.

Another anecdote involves a California recruiter who placed a regional sales manager with me. The recruiter was extremely efficient, checked references for me, did a lot of the leg work. About three months after I hired the candidate, a sharp guy with an engaging personality, it came to light that he was drawing paychecks from two companies at once, but not really working for either one. At that point, I double-checked his references and discovered that his entire resume was a work of fiction.

When I called the headhunter and discussed my concerns, he restated that the references had checked out. To make a long story short, he refused to refund the recruiting fee and our attorney recommended not even pursuing it due to the legal cost that would be involved. So, my bias is backed up by a fair amount of experience.

In reality, headhunters provide a valuable service. This is going to hurt some people to read this, but if human resources departments and hiring managers could do their jobs effectively, there wouldn't be any headhunters. But they can't, so there are. Headhunters have numerous techniques to find qualified candidates for a position. Some of the techniques would be illegal if performed by a hiring manager. For example, if the VP of Marketing from company A needed a qualified Marketing Manager and wanted to hire from his competitor, Company B, it would be illegal (tampering) to call that competitor and ask people to change jobs. But a headhunter can use marginally legitimate techniques to identify individuals within the competitive firm who might be receptive to making a job change.

John Lucht says that headhunters are acting only in their own best interest. It is difficult to say whether this is always accurate, but when you are unemployed, the headhunter will not be asking you to make a job change that isn't in your best interest. The key is to be cautious and only work with those recruiters who you know or who have excellent reputations. The risk of proliferation is inherent. If several headhunters submit your resume to a hiring manager in regard to a position, it simply doesn't look good. You might be disqualified for general suspicion.

There is a curious kind of catch 22 with headhunters. If you call a headhunter looking for a job, particularly when you are out of work, they don't often seem seriously interested to work with you. If they call you in regard to a position and you decline or hesitate, they will pursue you very hard. So, when you need them most is when headhunters do the least for you. And vice versa.

When my networking efforts generate the names of headhunters as leads, I generally don't call them. For the reasons above. I estimate that only about 10% of my interviews are the result of recruiters' efforts. If recruiters were particularly effective, that number would be closer to 50%. In spite of that, when a recruiter calls me, I always listen and then describe my goals to him/her. You never want to limit your sources of job leads.

Industrial Directories

There are numerous industrial directories or manufacturers' guides, most of which are available at your public library. Virtually every state has business directories listing the firms located in that state by SIC (Standard Industrial Classification), describing the firms' products, and providing the names of a few key executives, as well as addresses and phone numbers. Beyond that, there are specialized directories for various industries. The one I rely on, the *Medical Device Register*, is updated annually and provides tremendous information about the firms, their products, and the top managers.

In general, these are extraordinary sources of leads for cold calls. The best way to use them, as described in the setup section of this book, is to identify those firms which meet your basic choice criteria and begin contacting them. Those firms that do not have any appropriate opportunities will often become networking sources for you.

Attitude—Your Most Important Tool

Just how important is your attitude? The question can be answered by looking at how it impacts you in two ways—its importance to your commitment and how employers perceive it. Your attitude can become your most important asset in landing a job. It therefore must be extremely positive if you are to be successful.

Let's examine one particular scenario to see how your attitude might impact the results of your search. Assume for a moment that you've been out of work for about a month. Your search seems bogged down with no immediate relief in sight. It's a Wednesday morning and your alarm clock rings. What do you do? No matter how your spirits are down, no matter how unhappy you feel, no matter how much you'd rather go back to sleep, you have to resist that temptation and get up and begin the day's efforts toward finding a job. If your attitude is that of a defeatist, you'll simply find an excuse to go back to sleep rather than face the challenge. But you can't do that if you expect to land a good job offer today. You have to take control of your attitude.

How? Tough question, but there are ways to do it. One excellent way is to give yourself a pep talk. Say to yourself, loudly and enthusiastically, "I'm the one who has to make it happen. I'm the *only* one who can make it happen. I'm going to make it happen. If not today, soon, but it will be me in charge. I am the one. No one else is better at what I do!"

Maybe these aren't the exact words, but they are the precise sentiment. Tell yourself that you're the greatest. Shout it out loud and with feeling. (Don't be embarrassed if you give yourself a pep talk while you're driving in the car and other motorists are watching you.) You'll believe it if you say it aloud, and the outward projection of your attitude will say it to everyone you speak to. It's easy to feel sorry for yourself and stay in bed later than you should. It's easy to watch television and eat snacks all day. It's easy to be lazy and make excuses why you won't work on your job search until later. But you can make yourself feel good, to be in control, if you work at it.

Don't deny the truth. You can't fool yourself. Acknowledge that you need to find a good job and that it is a difficult task. Admit to yourself that you are in a demanding, stressful situation. Then give yourself a pep talk and move forward with *positive energy.* You'll feel better if you control your attitude and you'll be more successful in your job search.

How to keep your attitude positive

One of the best ways to maintain a positive attitude toward yourself and your job search is to make sure you feel good physically. (This applies all the time, not just when you need to find a job.) You can do that through proper diet and exercise. Follow the basic rules of healthy eating. Eat three healthy meals every day, avoiding fatty foods and excessive snacks. Get exercise on a regular basis. According to many cardiologists and other physicians, you should get at least twenty to thirty minutes of strenuous exercise every other day. Aerobics, jogging, bicycling, swimming, or whatever form of exercise you choose will allow you to become physically and mentally tougher. And you will need to be stronger to work through your job search. You will need the strength to keep a positive attitude in the face of difficult times and the likely disappointment if you don't find a job right away.

The key here is to force yourself to eat well and exercise three times per week. Most health professionals, by the way, recommend that you consult a physician before you embark upon any program of strenuous physical exercise. If you get adequate exercise, you'll feel better, you'll look better, you'll sleep better, and you'll be more capable of energetically dealing with the demands of your job search.

Another key component of the positive attitude is to keep yourself regimented, your time well structured. (This too applies all of the time, not just during your job search. But there's no reason you can't use the job search as an opportunity for self improvement.) If you set aside the time from 8 AM to 6 PM Monday through Friday, and use those hours exclusively for your search, you will be amazed at how much more you will accomplish and how much better you'll feel about yourself. You'll also be surprised at how much time you will find for the other activities in your life. You will find more time for activities such as working out, recreational reading, being with friends, or keeping your office space neat. Personally, I prefer to go to the gym at 6:30 AM so that I can hit my desk at 8:00 feeling invigorated.

Don't forget the pep talk as a key means of achieving a positive attitude. Whenever you start to feel down, give yourself a shot of enthusiasm by telling yourself how great you are. Remember that your attitude can change quickly in accordance with the events of the day, and you don't want that to work against you.

How your attitude is perceived

A hiring manager may make a judgement about you based on your attitude as much as on your qualifications. Let me rephrase that, so that the impact isn't lost. Your attitude, as perceived by a hiring manager, may be the most important judgement criteria in determining whether that manager wants to hire you. We all want to hire people we like, just as we all want to be hired by people we like. The attitude you project may be perceived as a key element of your personality. Are you
enthusiastic,
positive
outgoing
assured
confident
spirited
affirmative
optimistic
congenial
poised
any of dozens of other positive adjectives?

Or, do you project the image of being

dispassionate
vague
introverted
unsure
quiet
negative
secretive
confrontational
contrary
cynical
uncertain
any of dozens of other negative adjectives?

Do you view your job search as an opportunity and a
challenge which is
uplifting
interesting
exciting
enlightening
instructive?

Or do you view the search as
overwhelming
monotonous
oppressive
exhausting
terrifying
discouraging
depressing
tedious?

If you want to find the right job quickly, you better make

the right choice of attitude. When you feel your attitude slip into column B, it's time to give yourself a pep talk.

There are so many ways to be sure you project the right attitude. You've probably already become aware of many of these and you probably already act accordingly. Over time, you may have developed ways to project the most positive attitude you have. Your attitude shows in the way you dress, the way you style your hair, in your body language, in your speech habits, in the way you walk, and in everything you say and do.

You can't be sure how any given individual will perceive your attitude based upon a single input, but you can project an attitude that is positive, confident but not cocky, and comfortable. And when you feel your attitude start to slide, give yourself a pep talk. You want to be perceived positively.

Rule #12. Give yourself a pep talk whenever possible in order to keep yourself feeling positive and focused.

Looking at the negative side of attitude, consider how you might approach the situation as a hiring manager or decision maker. How do you think you would react to an individual who is negative, angry, or insecure? In a potential field of several candidates who all appear qualified on paper, the negative attitude is quickly eliminated from further consideration.

That candidate may have eliminated him/herself in the first five minutes of an interview. (The candidate with a negative attitude will usually receive a letter saying that the company has found another candidate with a more perfect match against the job requirements, but thanks for your interest. No one will tell you that your attitude is bad.) Most of us would not want to hire any one who might negatively affect others in the company. Nor would we want to hire any one who might be negative in interaction with others outside the company, giving the company a poor image.

The impact of others on your attitude

The people around you play a tremendous part in your attitude. Your family is likely to become discouraged at the time when you need their support most. What can you do? Let them know you're in control and give them a pep talk. Tell them how talented you are. Let them know that you need their assistance and support. Most of all, don't allow them to drag your attitude down.

Well wishing friends and relatives will call from time to time with the best of intentions. They want to offer their support and express their concern. The problem is that they often end up doing the opposite of what they intend. My father called me every week during one of my job searches, beginning the conversation with, "Well, do you have any news for me?" Of course he meant well, but I became angry with the same question week after week. I had to ask him to stop calling. The worst part of it is that it destroyed my attitude every time he called. The moral of the story is to be aware of the pitfalls of how friends and relatives impact your attitude.

The people you contact during your job search can also have a massive impact on your attitude. When you have an intellectually stimulating conversation with a hiring manager, it leaves you feeling stronger about yourself and motivates you to make more calls. This is true regardless of whether that manager has a potential job for you or not. On the other hand, when the people you call treat you negatively, your attitude can sag. And how you feel will be reflected in your next call. When this happens, take a five minute break and give yourself another pep talk. Remind yourself about the many successes you have had in your career, and begin with a fresh positive attitude.

The Interview

Yesss! You're finally getting your face in front of potential employers! When you reach the interview stage with any of the companies you have contacted, you have succeeded in demonstrating that you are a capable manager and, naturally, they're interested in speaking with you. This is a clear indication of a level of progress in your job search. Now is the time that control begins to shift away from the company and toward you. It is a critical time in the process, where you need to perform at peak efficiency. It is a time when the perceptions formed are of you the person, not of your resume or a set of faceless qualifications.

The interview process

It is important for you to think of the interview as part of a process, not as an isolated event. There are many ways that companies treat interviewing and the interview process; therefore you will have to succeed through each step of the process in order to arrive at your goal—an offer.

The interview process can be extremely short and simple. Some companies, for some jobs, will merely review resumes then make a hiring decision from a single interview involving a candidate meeting with only one manager. On the other extreme, some firms will require several batteries of interviews, each involving an interesting menu of different managers who have input into the final decision.

By the time the candidate gets to the offer stage, he/she will have met over a dozen individuals in the firm. Of course, there are numerous combinations and permutations of types and lengths of interview processes in between these extremes. Early in your first interview with each company, you should always ask about the interview process itself in order to better understand what the likely outcome of today will be. Ask how many interviews will be required and who is involved in each one.

My personal preference as a hiring manager is to begin the process with a brief telephone screening, followed by two personal interviews. If I am properly prepared as a hiring manager, I am confident that I can make smart decisions at that point in time. I generally involve only those others within my firm in the process whose specific input I need (if I have the latitude).

When to accept an interview

A smart candidate will not always accept an interview with a potential employer, but it is usually wise to schedule an interview at your (and the company's) earliest convenience when an employer expresses interest in seeing you. That is, unless you are clearly not interested in the company or the job. Even then, you might want to accept an interview just for the practice. Especially early in the job search, you may want to practice preparing for the interview and answering the tough questions that you should anticipate.

There is one particular set of circumstances that often

needs to be addressed at the time you accept an interview. That circumstance is the situation when you will need to travel, i.e. fly, to get to the interview and travel expenses will be incurred. It is customary for the employer to pay for your airfare when air travel is required, however some companies will not follow this practice. Politely, but explicitly, ask the person scheduling the interview what their procedure is for handling travel expenses during the interview process.

Some companies will send you the airline tickets prepaid or even put you in touch with their corporate travel agent so that arrangements can be made and billed directly to the company. This allows the company to control your travel expenditure, while minimizing their paperwork. Some companies will even arrange to have your hotel and rental car billed directly to the company. Many smaller companies, having less sophisticated organizations, will ask you to buy the tickets (charge them on your credit card) and then submit the expenses for reimbursement. This usually works fine, although I can think of one notable exception.

About a month after I had submitted my expenses to the hiring manager, and having not received a reimbursement check, I called just to make certain that the receipts had not been lost in the mail. The manager told me he hadn't opened his mail yet. What? Can you imagine working for a manager who doesn't open his mail for a month? That would be an ongoing nightmare. It's a good thing I didn't get the job. Anyhow, two weeks later, my check finally arrived via Federal Express.

If a company asks you to pay for and absorb your own airfare with no reimbursement, this is a red flag and you probably won't want to accept the interview. After all, what kind of company would operate this way, and how do they treat their employees? This effectively becomes a control issue, and this is a time you should take control by politely declining.

Some managers, or their secretaries, will offer an interview at a specific date and time. There is generally a good reason for this specificity and, consequently, you should accept it unless you have an unreconcilable scheduling conflict. In that situation, you should politely ask for an alternative date and time.

Other managers will suggest a specific date and allow you to choose the time. My experience says you can maximize the use of your time if you take an early morning appointment so that you can travel early and not use an entire day for two or three hours of interviews. You will also find that the early morning is a better time of day to meet with someone, due to the fact that his/her mind will not be cluttered by the events of the day and they will be better able to focus on you. The second best time is right after lunch, when they will be feeling more energetic. In fact, on a second or third interview you may want to have a lunch interview in order to get the manager out of the office and into a more relaxed environment.

In still other cases, an interested hiring manager may indicate an interest in seeing you and leave the date and time up to you. It is my opinion, and it has been my experience, that you should schedule your interview for the soonest date possible. Delays will not enhance your chances. But take charge and suggest two or three alternative dates and times. Let him/her know you are decisive.

How to prepare for an interview

Absolutely the first thing you must do in preparing for an interview is to define an objective. No matter what else you do you need to have an achievable goal for every interview. That is the only way you can successfully close an interview or to have a means of measuring whether you've been successful or not. For example, your goal might be to get invited back for a second interview. Or if this is the final interview in the process, your objective would likely be to get a job offer. There are other possible scenarios as well. For example, someone involved in the interview process may have told you that no one gets hired without meeting the president first, so being invited back for an interview with the president may be your goal. Regardless of the situation, you must have a clear objective.

Another key element of preparing for the interview is planning for your physical appearance. Everyone knows the importance of a good appearance, but plan it in advance so you won't be left short.

Make sure you get a haircut or get your hair styled before the interview if you will need it. Make sure that your shoes are shined. Go to the dry cleaner and pick up your shirts, suit, dress, etc. the day before your interview. And men, be certain your tie matches your suit.

The next element of preparation is to anticipate questions that will be asked of you and prepare sharp, direct responses. Read over your resume (have extra copies of the correct resume with you) and look for potential questions that will be asked:

Why did you leave your last job? Have positive answers. What are your strong points? Don't be modest; memorize a comprehensive list.

What are your weaknesses? Never admit any major ones. Only acknowledge vague irrelevant weaknesses. An example of this is "I'd like to read more." Never inadvertently talk anyone out of hiring you. (It happens all too often).

What are you looking for? Remember your ultimate goal; describe it in a way that relates to this company and this job. Be decisive.

What do you like most about work? Have a comprehensive answer.

What do you like least about work? Mention something minor.

Again, don't inadvertently eliminate yourself.

You will also want to do your homework on the company where you are interviewing. Use the library, other employees, competitors, customers, even call and ask for an annual report and product literature. The more you know, the better you will fare in your interview. You will not be expected to be an expert, only to be reasonably prepared so that you have some prior knowledge and a written list of questions you will want to answer during the interview. Yes, a written list of questions. Generally, these will become more specific as you move through the interview process.

The questions you ask will vary depending upon the type of job you are seeking, but they should reflect a long term interest in the company. Questions about the company's commitment to research and development, their growth rate over the last five years, the number of employees, likely acquisitions, new products, new markets, etc. will demonstrate your interest in the company beyond the next paycheck. Ask questions about the company and its officers, its products, its customers, and the job. Show an interest that goes beyond the scope of the specific job you are interviewing for. Show them that you are a thoughtful, thorough person.

References are eventually going to be requested if a job offer is to be made. A request for references is usually a buying sign. Therefore, you should make up a list of several references. They can be previous supervisors, customers, vendors, employees who you have supervised, or any other relevant individuals who know you and some aspect of your background. Before you give this list to anyone, though, call each person on your list and ask if they are willing to serve as references for you. Don't use anyone as a reference unless he/she will say positive things about you. The hiring managers want to hear affirmative comments at this stage of the process.

Planning your travel to the interview site is a key part of your pre-interview preparation. Particularly if your travel is by car, determine how long it will take you to travel to your destination and make sure you get there adequately in advance of your scheduled interview time, planning for potential delays. If you arrive early, find a convenient hotel or other public place nearby and use the restroom and phone facilities so that you get to your meeting looking fresh and ready to shine.

The last preparation step will probably take place in the car in the parking lot outside of the interview. *Give yourself another pep talk.* You want to be really "up" when you walk in that door, so spend about two minutes on this pep talk. Act enthusiastic and you'll be enthusiastic! It's contagious. It will pay huge dividends.

Many people are fearful or apprehensive about interviews. Whether your job routinely involves meeting the public may impact how you feel going into the interview. A sales person, for example, is involved in "interviews" every day as a routine part of the selling job. If your job requires public or customer contact on a regular basis, you will probably be less nervous about the interview than if your job does not involve public contact, such as an internal financial or technical responsibility. It's common sense that you will feel most comfortable doing what you usually do.

It's okay to be a little nervous; it won't hurt your job chances. But if you appear panic-stricken, you may eliminate yourself from serious consideration. The best way to avoid this is to practice. Make a list of questions you would be expected to answer (and the answers you will give) and a list of questions you would like to ask a perspective employer. Practice in front of a mirror or practice with a friend or associate. Go on a couple of interviews, even those where you know you are not qualified for the job. The practice will help you feel more confident, and you may get an unexpected offer. If you are severely challenged by the thought of an interview, get professional help. There are agencies who can help prepare you for the process.

Your demeanor during the interview

There are volumes of material written about how to conduct yourself once you are in an interview. My personal preference is to remember three words:

Focus!

Enthusiasm!

Smile!

I repeat these words to myself at strategic times during the interview. *Focus* on what the interviewer is saying and the questions that are being asked. Do not allow your mind to wander. Sometimes, one of the managers you meet in a series of interviews may be extremely boring (and bored). That manager can still give you plenty of insight into the company as well as influencing the decision regarding your hire. Maintain your focus and intensity.

You can demonstrate your *enthusiasm* for yourself, your job, and your company in a number of ways. Verbal cues are the easiest to read. Speak in a spirited manner and use action words whenever possible. Real action verbs such as

drive,
initiate,
motivate,
launch,

and countless others will demonstrate your enthusiasm. Bland verbs such as

made,
worked,
started

are more passive and do not reflect enthusiasm. Still, a lively tone of voice will convey enthusiasm regardless of the words you choose.

You can also show enthusiasm in your body language. The shelves of your local library have numerous writings on this subject. But a few basic rules are easy to remember. Sit erect leaning slightly forward in your chair, do not cross your arms or legs, use limited hand gestures, and make frequent eye contact with your interviewer. It is helpful to appear confident, but not too relaxed. Use your body language to convey a positive message to an employer, that you are an enthusiastic person (which is contagious) and that you are enthusiastic about their company and job. People like to work with others who are enthusiastic.

You will also want to make an ongoing evaluation of the interviewer's body language. The information contained therein will tell you a great deal about the impression you are making. If the manager is not making eye contact, ask a question or make a statement beginning with his/her first name to be sure you have their full attention. If the manager is sitting with his/her arms crossed, they either don't believe you or are bored by what you are saying. Put more enthusiasm in your voice to get their attention. Be excited and they will be excited about you. If the interviewer keeps looking at his/her watch, ask if they have a time constraint. That way, you will create a positive image of being considerate and the interviewer will have a comfortable means of ending the interview if necessary and sending you to the next person. Or, it will tell them that you are attentive and will force them to focus on you. In many situations, the interviewer is distracted and needs help in focusing on the candidate. Body language is a two way street.

The one ingredient which makes a strong first impression and also conveys a positive, enthusiastic image is a *smile*. If you smile when you are introduced to someone, you make a much more positive impression. Look at it from the other side—a candidate who wants to work for you and arrives for an interview looking insipid and uninterested has started off on the wrong foot. Would you hire a candidate who doesn't give a positive first impression? That's how important your smile is. A significant part of the hire/don't hire decision is formulated in the first few seconds when a manager meets a candidate.

Beyond the initial smile, you should continue to smile at appropriate times during the interview. And make it a genuine smile, not a phony looking grin. Even an appropriate laugh during an interview will help to create a bond between you and the interviewer.

There is clearly more to interviewing well than focus, enthusiasm, and smile. If you are well prepared, you will have anticipated many of the questions asked and you should have decisive answers prepared. Answer in a clear voice, using good volume—neither too loud nor too soft.

If the hiring manager asks you a difficult question that may require additional research, answer honestly that you will find the answer and get the information to him/her.

When a question is asked and your answer clearly will not help your chances in landing the job, be direct and refocus on a strength after briefly acknowledging the deficiency.

When the answer to a question will definitely enhance your likelihood of achieving your goal, expand upon the answer so that the interviewer will not be able to overlook your obvious strength. After answering the question, ask the interviewer for agreement that this is important. You may do that by simply asking, "Is that an important consideration for the person you hire for this job?" Make that manager say yes as many times as possible in regard to your qualifications. That will help make the answer yes when you ask for the job.

When the interviewer is less than fully prepared, you may hit some dead spots in the interview. These are the pregnant pauses where no one seems to know quite what to say. You should be ready to take control by asking one of your prepared questions at this point. If you are unsure of what to say, ask about the interview process.

How many interviews are usually required?
How many candidates do you plan to see?
When do you want to fill the job?

The answers to these questions will generally regain the focus and attention of the interviewer, while helping you ease through those pregnant pauses.

Ending the interview can be awkward and difficult. There are numerous ways to exit, but I would recommend the following. If the interviewer takes the lead and tells you what will happen next, or when you will hear something, follow that lead.

Whether he/she does that or not, summarize what you consider to be the three major reasons why you could and should be selected to move to the next step in the interview process or be given an offer. Tell him/her that you're excited about the opportunity and the company and ask when you will hear from him/her again. That will allow you to know when to take the next follow up step if you don't hear from them first. Close by asking for the job. The higher your position within the organization, the more subtlety you should use. As a sales rep, you will be expected to ask for the job. It is a means of demonstrating your skill. As an executive, a more indirect close is needed.

Follow up to the personal interview

You must be aware that follow up can make the difference when a hiring manager must choose between two candidates who are very close in qualifications. Follow up can even make the ultimate difference in a hiring decision, particularly when your post interview communication reflects well on the quality and thorough nature of the work that you perform.

There are several types of follow up which may be required after your interview. The first and most immediate need is a written note thanking the interviewer, confirming your continuing interest based upon the interview, and noting the fact that you are excited, well qualified, and ready to move along in the process. As I mentioned previously, you should probably write a creative letter for this purpose on the word processor, store it in memory, and customize it as needed. The follow up letter should be reasonably brief—three short paragraphs—and explicit.

Paragraph 1: Thank you, the job is exciting.

Paragraph 2: Three key reasons why you should be given the job.

Paragraph 3: Thanks again, I'm excited, I look forward to hearing from you (or seeing you) again.

When should you use this letter? Every time you have an interview, and with every person you meet, including secretaries who may have been instrumental in arranging your interviews or people who have no input into the hiring decision. You should mail this letter the same day as the interview if possible, or the next morning. In urgent or hot situations, you may send a Western Union Mailgram or Federal Express letter instead. I would, by the same token, recommend against sending a follow up letter by fax because of the impersonal nature of a fax. Anyone can read it, not just the person it is addressed to.

This does not have to be the first means of follow up you employ. A simple little trick that a headhunter taught me can also be very useful. He suggested that I leave a brief hand written letter, in a sealed envelope, at the reception desk when I was leaving, so that the interviewer would get immediate feedback from me. Doing this will set you apart from the other candidates that are being interviewed. I would recommend that you follow that with the mailed letter described in the previous paragraphs.

Okay, so you had a successful interview. You left a hand written note at the reception desk and you sent a formal follow up letter in the mail the next morning. You were specifically told that you would hear from them within two weeks. Two weeks come and go, no contact—What should you do? You don't want to lose momentum and you don't want to seem pushy, so what is the next step? Have you been in that situation? The answer to what to do is that you have to be tenacious and take the bull by the horns. Make the phone call! Simply tell the hiring manager that, based upon what you were told in the interview, you had expected to hear from them by now, and that you want to call as a follow up and to reiterate that you are excited about the job. Tell them you know you can get great results in the position. They may think you're a little pushy, but more likely they will consider you a determined individual, the kind they want for the job.

Regardless of the exact scenario, you must take control. Always ask when you can expect the next contact from the company. This assists you in keeping your expectations realistic, while also giving you a timetable for your next follow up. You should make explicit notes in your word processor—you remember this from the set-up section, don't you?—so that you will know what follow up steps are needed every morning when you sit down at your desk. Sometimes, the next step for you will be a phone call. Sometimes, you may owe them information they requested from the previous interview. Other times you will send additional follow up letters.

Feedback from employers

Verbal messages and written formats including form letters comprise the feedback you get from employers. To the candidate, there never seems to be enough feedback. And when you get it, the feedback always seems to be painful. When you're unemployed and looking for a job, your psyche is in its most delicate state. Most of the feedback you get will either be rejection or non-specific.

Non-specific feedback may take the form of what I call the form non-rejection letter. You've probably seen these or you soon will. They say thanks for the resume, we're reviewing it and will call you if there is a fit. It is a *de facto* rejection, but carefully avoids mentioning that reality.

Rejection, as a form of feedback, is not what you wanted to hear. You want an employer to be impressed with your credentials, to schedule an interview, and to make you a good job offer. But so many employers don't seem to even have the courtesy, or intestinal fortitude, to extend you a written or spoken rejection.

Many managers will simply discontinue communicating with you when they have determined that they no longer want to pursue you as a candidate for a job. The result of this is that you keep making fruitless phone calls and the hiring manager continues expending energy avoiding you. This is usually more frustrating than receiving a written rejection letter. And it tends to give you hope, albeit false hope in many instances. As painful as rejection may be, it clearly signals an endpoint. Simply being ignored by an employer is far worse.

I would recommend that you keep the lines of communication open until the door is slammed shut. Stay in touch until you get specific feedback. Sometimes, rejection is based upon a misconception or misunderstanding. In those cases, you may want to follow up with a hiring manager after you have been rejected. It is possible to reopen the case by clarifying a misunderstanding.

Personal interviews will usually result in some form of feedback rather than your being ignored. The manager generally feels compelled to give the candidate a response after an interview. Phone calls and letters are treated more casually.

Feedback is one area where recruiters provide a valuable input into the process. An employer and a candidate can communicate through a recruiter quite frankly. The recruiter can filter the inputs in both directions to minimize feelings getting hurt. In addition, recruiters will provide that necessary communication link because it is in their interest as well.

The Offer

This could potentially be the shortest chapter of this book. Still, there is some valuable information to be imparted on this subject. There is a basic tendency for most people to end their job search as soon as they receive an offer. Please don't do this. Why? For several reasons:

The offer may not be good enough.
You may want to negotiate a better compensation package.
You may want to negotiate a better relocation package.
You may receive other offers.
The company may not be right for you.
The job may not be right for you.

Rule #13. Never accept an offer without taking a brief time to consider the position from all viewpoints.

So what should you do? When you receive an offer from an employer, immediately thank them for the offer and ask for some time to consider the merits of the offer (or talk it over with your spouse if you are married.) How long? Depending on your level within the organization, you should indicate anywhere from a couple of days to a week. Even if you feel that it is the most fantastic job at a great salary in a great company, you will do yourself a favor if you wait at least twenty-four hours before you accept. This accomplishes two things. First, it shows that you are a reflective, careful person and, consequently, reconfirms to the company that they made a good choice in extending the offer to you instead of another candidate.

Second, it gives you time to evaluate the offer fairly to make sure it is right for you and to determine if you want to renegotiate any portion of the package. No hiring manager will be offended if you ask for a little time to give serious consideration to the offer. If you have doubts, tell the employer that it sounds like a great offer, but you want a couple of days to carefully evaluate it.

Remember, when you receive an offer, *you are now in total control of the decision process.*

The longer you have been out of work the greater the temptation will be to accept an offer that is not quite as good as it should be. If you've been off the payroll for several months, the temptation may be greater to accept a subpar offer. After all, it seems logical that a job at 80% of what you're accustomed to receiving is far better than nothing. The risk of buying into this logic is that you may accept a job where you'll become dissatisfied in the short term future. And then you might be tempted to begin another job search. As inviting as this offer may be, it is not always in your best interest nor is it fair to the employer.

How do you avoid this pitfall? After you have received an offer, your attitude will be sky high. This is a great time to close the loop with other employers on your list who seem to be sitting on the fence with a decision. You might find that you'll get one or more other offers for comparison. Then you can make a great choice.

What if everything's good except the salary? After taking time to consider the offer, tell the employer that you think it is an excellent offer and you'd like to accept it with a higher salary (be specific). Even if they cannot offer you more money, they will not withdraw the offer because you asked for a higher salary. They will respect you for it. They will feel more sure they want you on their side in business. The initial offer is your best opportunity to get more money. Once you are on board, what do you think they would say if you asked for more salary? Right! Also, make sure that you know what your decision will be, based upon the realm of possible responses to your request for more money. If they give you only a portion of the additional compensation you requested, will you accept?

In most cases, I have found that there is a 10-15% flex in the initial offer and some employers may even expect you to ask for more, depending upon the type of job and your level in the organization. In other cases, you may be able to negotiate a higher base salary in exchange for a reduced bonus opportunity.

You can also negotiate other perquisites—yes, that is the proper unabridged term for perks—when you have received an offer. For example, I once negotiated three weeks vacation the first year when I had received an offer. My rationale was that I had three weeks at my present employer and I preferred not to backpedal. They gave it to me without hesitation. I also negotiated a higher starting salary, about 7%, from that employer.

Finally, ask to receive the offer in writing. This will protect you and the employer from disputes that might arise later, and it will protect you if you are currently employed and need to resign your present position first.

But be amply prepared for buyer's remorse—the situation where you convince yourself that you made a mistake, after you have made an acceptance decision. It's normal to have those second thoughts even if you consider it an ideal job situation. You may have felt the same thing when you bought a new car. Don't let temporary doubts get in the way of going to work!

Inescapably, we should discuss the counter offer. Some candidates, less than sincere in their interest to find a new job, will use a prospective employer's offer as a means of generating a counter offer from their present employer. This is not a recommended tactic. In other situations, submitting your resignation will result in your receiving an unexpected counter-offer from your present employer. The general rule is not to accept a counter offer from your present employer. You will always be perceived as a traitor and, consequently, you will be eliminated from consideration for future promotions. You may get what you want in the short run, but you will lose out in the long run.

Miscellaneous Topics

Cattle calls

Some employers who are indecisive want to feel triply sure before making a job offer to a prospective candidate. In order to increase their comfort level with the eventual hiring decision, they will parade a huge number of "qualified candidates" before the hiring managers. This is the way some companies and managers overcome self doubt. Have you ever been in a hiring situation where the interviewing manager tells you that they want to look at fifteen or twenty candidates before they narrow the field to a few finalists? It's extremely frustrating. This is what is known as a cattle call. They want to look at the entire herd before selecting the animal for the slaughter, er... I mean job.

The dynamics of the cattle call are interesting. It may take the hiring managers several days or even several weeks to find time in their schedules to see all of the candidates. How productive can they be in performing their other job related responsibilities during that time? Furthermore, do you think that many managers are capable of accurately recalling the specifics of a large number of interviews over a period of days or weeks in order to make an informed decision? Even if they take copious notes, it is unlikely that they will remember more than two or three candidates.

And who will they remember? They will be able to recall the first candidate they saw, the last candidate, and any unusual candidates or circumstances. As an example, if you are seven feet tall, they will remember you. Or if you discovered you have close friends in common with one of the managers, or went to the same school as one of them, he/she will remember you. There is no doubt that adequate pre-screening would prevent most hiring managers from having to live through the time consuming ordeal of the cattle call. And they would eliminate having to put their best candidates through the same trial and tribulation.

You can react to the cattle call in two ways. If you have asked, and a hiring manager indicates there will be a large number of candidates, you may decline the interview. You may choose to consider it a hopelessly negative situation and use your time pursuing other opportunities. Or, if you think it is an excellent job in an outstanding company, you may try to schedule yourself as either the first or the last interview. That would be to your advantage.

You may also attempt a little bit of salesmanship. Find a showy way to separate yourself from the other candidates in the mind of the hiring managers. An unusual presentation of your qualifications may get the job done. For example, make a stand-up display with each of your key credentials in bold print on a separate page. Do something which makes you different from the other candidates. You must avoid appearing crass, gaudy, or unsophisticated, but the creative candidate can find a way to distinguish him/herself.

There is one other possible approach to the cattle call interview. Assume it is hopeless and use it as an opportunity to polish up your interviewing skills. If you should happen to get invited to a second interview, consider it a bonus.

Gender

Gender plays a major role in the way you interact with the principals of any company during the job search. Your own gender can work for you or against you, depending upon the inner prejudices of the hiring manager. Just as a hiring manager has a bias towards particular types of experience, that manager probably has a preference as to whether a male or a female would be best for the job. That bias can be the result of affirmative action, prejudice, or any number of mind-set elements. These mental limitations of hiring managers are beyond your control.

On the other hand, how you relate to gender is completely within your control and can be used to your advantage. You can eliminate gender bias from your speech and your written communication, which will improve your chances of being accepted. A specific example of this would be the cover letter you send in response to a newspaper ad.

Consider an ad that instructs you to write to the attention of T. Smith. How do you know if T. Smith is a man or a woman? If T. Smith is a woman, and you write to Mr. T. Smith with a greeting of Dear Mr. Smith, Ms. Smith might be displeased enough to disqualify you from further consideration. The best way to handle the situation is to simply address the letter to T. Smith and use the greeting of Dear Mr./Ms. Smith. This is gender neutral and you will probably not offend anyone with this approach and you will not harm your chances. Or in response to an ad without a contact name, the greeting might be "Dear Ladies/Gentlemen." (In responding to an ad without a contact name, you may want to blindly call the company and ask for the name of the person whose title you are addressing your letter to.)

These are simple examples of how gender sensitivity can work in your favor or against you. There are many similar situations which occur frequently during your job search. You should always be sensitive to gender and use it to your benefit.

Getting through on the phone

One of the potentially difficult and frustrating repetitive challenges during your job search is reaching the person you want on the telephone. It is often difficult to get past the screen that is erected by the receptionist or secretary. The challenge is to turn the person behind that screen into an ally, not an adversary.

Let's start with an understanding of why the screen is there. It is there primarily because the company's top management wants to limit the access of cold callers to the employees in order to minimize interruptions to their work. When you are calling on a referral from your network, it is usually easier to get through by mentioning the name of the referring individual. When you are cold calling the president of a company, or a vice president for that matter, the receptionist or secretary will ask what company you are calling from. Well, you aren't calling from a company, so what do you say? Tell them that you are not affiliated with a firm. This may make it more difficult for you to get through.

But if you are speaking with an uncooperative receptionist, ask to be connected to the hiring manager's secretary. The receptionist will usually accede to your wishes. When you reach the secretary, let him/her know that you are calling about employment and be specific about the type of job you are seeking. Usually, the secretary will either give your message to the boss, or simply refer you to a more appropriate manager to assist you. Always ask for the secretary's name, record it, and employ your best etiquette.

There may be situations when you do not know the name of the manager you need to reach. On these occasions, you may want to call and ask the receptionist for the name of the individual who holds the title you are trying to reach. The receptionist will give you that individual's name most of the time.

Sometimes, you will be referred to the Human Resources, aka Personnel Department. Depending upon the company, this may be a dead end, so probe to determine if this is actually the best route for your entree into the company. I call this a potential dead end, not to insult human resources professionals, but to reflect the reality that the decisions are usually made by the department where you will ultimately work. Human Resources will often ask for a resume, then send you either a rejection letter or a non-specific response. This is because they may not recognize the specific qualities you possess that a department manager might want. (See the Human Resources section later in this book).

When you finally reach the manager you seek to contact, you must be prepared to briefly tell him/her why you are calling and to describe your abilities in one or two sentences.

Be persistent on the telephone. It may take you a dozen or more phone calls to reach your intended party. Be prepared to continue calling until you have made contact. As long as it is not a toll call, you won't be wasting your money or effort. Do your best to sound enthusiastic on the phone. Develop a telephone relationship with that receptionist or secretary so that he/she will assist you in getting through and leaving messages. The ease of getting through to the correct manager or executive the first time is not necessarily related to your eventual likelihood of getting a job offer.

Unusual questions you may be asked on an interview.

No matter how you prepare for the questions you may be asked on an interview, there may be some that you cannot anticipate. You must be able to answer these questions successfully. The hiring manager wants to see how you think on your feet. You can expect questions about what you have accomplished, why you left a company, what you want to do, what your strengths and weaknesses are.

Still, you may be asked a few questions which you could not anticipate. Every hiring manager seems to have a different style. As a hiring manager, my personal preference is to determine ahead of time what I want to know and what criteria I will use to judge the candidates. Then I simply ask questions that will tell me what I want to know—questions about what the candidate has accomplished, or questions which encourage the candidate to speak freely so that I can learn what kind of person he/she is. This allows me to get to know the candidates a little bit as business professionals and as people. It works for me. But let's consider some of the types of interviewer you may have the occasion to meet.

The Unprepared Interviewer. This manager will appear unprepared, having little or no prior knowledge of you or your resume, incomplete information about the job, and precious few questions to ask. In order to cover for this, the unprepared interviewer will often begin by asking if you have any questions. The unfortunate side to this is the negative way it colors your perception of the company. It certainly gives you the impression that the company is not interested in you.

If this manager is your potential supervisor in the company, it may have serious impact on your continued level of interest in the job. As difficult as it may seem, you must attempt to impress this person. The best way to respond is to have probing, perceptive questions prepared regarding the company and the job to let them know that your interest is serious. You may also want to ask that individual questions about his/her role in the firm's business.

The Amateur Psychologist. On occasion, you will be asked questions which are behavioral in nature, rather than being specific about you and your background. This interviewer may feel that he/she is capable of drawing conclusions about your psychological makeup from your answers to a few questions. The truth is that this manager is fooling him/herself. A certified psychologist or psychiatrist would require hours of meetings and far more information to draw the conclusions this manager is trying to infer from your answers to a few brief questions.

How do you respond to the amateur psychologist? Answer the questions the best way you can. In this situation, I have been tempted to sarcastically ask the questioner about his/her experience in the field of psychology. However, if your questions are misinterpreted or misconstrued, you will damage your chances of moving along in the process. Remember to exercise your control here. Refer to Rule #10.

The Format Questioner. We have all been in interviews that tend to follow an impersonal pattern of questions, most often in opposite pairs. These questions probably don't give the hiring manager much information about you. This usually reflects a limitation of the interviewer, but once again the candidate must bear with it, since the interviewer is largely in control here, even though it does not provide much information to either party. The questions might be:

What are your strengths?
What are your weaknesses?
What do you like the most about your job?
What do you like the least about your job?
What accomplishment are you most proud of in your career?
What are you least proud of in your career?
What kind of management style do you like the best?
What kind of management style do you like the least?
Ad infinitum.

There is nothing wrong with this type of interview, but it is certainly unimaginative. And you should have answers prepared for this type of question. Answer the questions honestly and thoroughly. Then ask the questions that will provide you with the information you will need to make a decision.

The Moocher. This individual gets his/her name from the fact that he/she seems to want something for nothing. I have run across this situation twice over the years and I feel angry whenever I look back upon those two interviews. What happens is that the hiring manager asks the candidate to write a business plan or a launch plan, which is relevant to the company's future, as preparation for the interview.

On the first occasion, I spent two days preparing a detailed plan absent enough knowledge to be truly effective. An effective plan requires intense familiarity with the business. I didn't get the job. The second time I was asked for a plan, my response was to suggest that it is impossible to do that with my limited knowledge of the specifics. The manager asked me to do it anyway. I said that I thought it was unfair to ask me to spend several hours on a plan that he should have written himself. Needless to say, I disqualified myself from consideration. My feeling was, and is, that this is merely an exercise and that no one should get something for nothing. If a manager expects you to perform in this way just to get an interview, what would he/she ask you to do after you were hired? Would you want to work for this kind of manager?

The Human Resources Department

The Human Resources department is a vital part of most large companies. However, hiring is not always their forte. They are often more intensely involved in benefits, relocation packages, and developmental programs. Usually, they provide hiring assistance to the hiring manager in one of a few ways. Sometimes, they perform the recruitment function, providing the hiring manager with an agenda of qualified applicants. They may do this by using a recruiter, by placing an ad in appropriate periodicals, or by searching within the firm for interested, qualified candidates. They may conduct an initial screening.

Or in some cases, the HR manager may be part of a battery of interviews. Every company has its own procedures. Inevitably, the HR manager may be the one to extend an offer to the chosen candidate and will be actively involved in all negotiations. Still, the hiring decision is usually made by the manager of the appropriate department.

What happens if you make your initial contact with the HR Department? This is certainly appropriate when an ad asks you to do so. But if you start in HR in cold call situations, you may end up missing out on many opportunities such as those which are thus far unofficial and consequently HR is not yet in the cycle.

The key is to become involved with HR after it has been determined that you are nominally qualified for a position. The hiring manager may at that time refer your resume to HR for processing. Starting in HR, however, is usually a dead end. Why? Because Human Resources is deluged with unrequested resumes. The best they can usually do is acknowledge receipt of the resume and either forward it to the functional manager or keep it on file. If you are a sales manager, the Vice President of Sales will be the most beneficial manager to see your resume first. If you are an engineer, the VP of Engineering is the one. They are better equipped to evaluate the experience on your resume and make a go/no go decision.

The moral of the story is to avoid making contact with Human Resources until you have explored the needs of the functional area where you wish to work. It can't always be done, but try try try.

The ideal candidate

As you move through the job search, you will often hear managers speak of the ideal candidate. For the most part, they do not expect to find the ideal candidate, but many hiring managers will not let go of the belief that their elusive stereotype actually exists. It can become a source of frustration to an employer to engage in the never-ending search for that perfect match of skills, personality, experience, and availability. In the worst cases, I have seen hiring managers leave positions unfilled for months and months as the search for the ideal candidate continues. Still, as the job seeker, you can become victimized by the uncertainty which some managers show in continuing to seek that elusive perfect fit.

It becomes your responsibility to let hiring managers know that you are imperfect, but extremely well-suited for a position. Make them focus on your accomplishments. The key element of the search for the ideal candidate, however, is for you—the job seeker—to know when to let go of an opportunity and dedicate your time to pursuing other job opportunities you may have identified.

You may encounter the situation where the employer has not rejected you, but will not commit to moving you further along in the process. This can be severely discouraging. If the hiring manager has indicated that they must have the ideal candidate, you need to take control. How? Make a simple pitch explaining how much you can accomplish in the job, showing how closely you match up against the job requirements. Explain once again how well your background matches their needs. Then ask for the job in a strong way. "Don't you agree that I'm capable of getting the results you want and more?" Pause... Wait... Be prepared to wait as long as necessary for an answer, making eye contact all the while.

Use that silence to force the manager to think. And to answer. If you still get a no, summarize once again and let them know that the ball is in their court. Make a judgement whether you need to follow up or let go. Are they going to keep you hanging and "settle for second best" if the ideal candidate doesn't materialize? The ideal candidate probably doesn't exist.

Discussing money

One topic which comes up frequently during your job search is money. Specifically, how much you want to make in your next job. One of the critical elements of self evaluation is to determine how much you should be expecting to earn in your new job. Having done that prior to beginning your search, you need to determine when it is appropriate to discuss money during the interview process.

Like so many other aspects of the job search, there is no clear cut answer to when you should discuss money. Or even when to answer questions about money. Going back to the beginning of your job search, how much did you determine you are worth? Most of us feel that, realistically, we should earn as much as we were paid at our last job, or slightly more. In the real world, let's examine the alternatives: If you are seeking less money, there had better be extenuating circumstances or you may need to reexamine your sense of self worth. If you are seeking substantially more than you have previously earned, you must likewise be prepared to totally justify why you are worth so much more. How will you fare compared to other candidates? It's okay to say you expect a little more than other candidates may ask for—that probably won't hurt your chances of getting an offer—but you will need to be able to amply warrant a request for a substantially higher salary.

So when do you discuss money? It's a judgement call. But consider the fact that most of the candidates for a position are looking for a salary in the same range. Consider the fact that the employer knows this and probably has a predetermined salary range for the position. If the hiring manager asks how much compensation you are looking for, you have only two alternatives. The first, obviously, is to tell him/her how much you expect to earn based upon previous earnings and future expectations. The second is to avoid a direct answer to the question. I have personally taken the second alternative many times when I feel confident that I am in the range.

You can defer answering the question by saying, "I'm certain that I'm in the salary range for the job." In the absence of that certainty, you may instead say, "I hope you don't mind, but I feel that it's premature to discuss money. I would prefer not to prejudice you one way or the other at this point." Or, "I'm sure that my expectations fall within your salary range for the position." Most hiring managers will respect your feelings on this. By the way, this may be a good time to ask the salary range for the job.

Another option is to respond to questions about earning expectations by using the opportunity to find where you fit in their decision process. When asked how much you are seeking, respond with a question, such as "Does this mean you're ready to discuss an offer?" But please don't sound sarcastic doing this.

You may choose to ask about money before the hiring manager does so. My personal preference is not to do so until I have moved reasonably far along in the process. There is some risk inherent in avoiding such a discussion, however. In one particular situation, I had flown from the east coast to Seattle to interview for a job with an exceptionally strong company known for its unusual management style. On the second trip, I asked about the compensation range for the job only to be truly disappointed by the fact that the salary was below my acceptable range and apparently didn't have any flex. I had wasted two trips, two long and gruelling trips, to interview for a job where I was seeking compensation significantly above the predetermined starting salary.

So you can see the risk of not asking. But, because money should not be the primary concern, it can be detrimental to ask prematurely. It may work for you to simply ask about the generalities of the compensation plan—do its components include:

salary,
bonus,
commission,
stock,
profit sharing?

On the other hand, if you presume that the job, because of its level in a competitive marketplace, will have an appropriate compensation package, it is perfectly okay to postpone discussing money until the end. You may actually strengthen your position by doing so. If the employer really wants you for the job, and if the hiring manager eliminates the other candidates from consideration, you should be able to reach a compromise.

The ultimate answer to the question of when to discuss money is whenever you feel comfortable doing it. It helps an employer as well as a candidate to be attuned to one another in this regard.

Just make sure you understand the strengths and weaknesses of each approach.

The waiting game

Sometimes, it takes an incredibly long time for an employer to give you feedback after an interview. How to deal with waiting is a real challenge. Even if you have followed up in writing and by telephone, there are times when the process takes so long or becomes so bogged down that it seems as if a decision will never be made. This situation is often related to a cattle call. My rule for determining what the likely outcome will be is quite simple: Good decisions are made quickly, bad decisions take a long time. Almost without exception this has proven to be true.

If an employer is going to make you an offer or move you to the next stage of the process, it usually happens fairly soon. If they are unsure, they will delay for a long time until eliminating you from consideration. They probably knew early in the process that you were not the candidate that they were seeking. But they lacked the resolve to admit it to themselves. It is best to assume it is a dead issue in these situations, when the employer has allowed several weeks to pass without a decision. In the event that you are wrong, you will be pleasantly surprised and presumably pleased to move along in the process. If you are correct, which is usually the case, you will have avoided false expectations and thus committed your efforts elsewhere.

You may be familiar with the situation described above. It occurs when you have had an apparently successful interview, but received only vague feedback from the employer afterward. The first solid feedback you receive, over the phone, is that there is one more candidate who must be evaluated first before a decision is made. The employer has not acknowledged that you are no longer a viable candidate, but it is evident that you would have received a positive response if you were. That other candidate, brought in late, will invariably get the nod. For some reason, the employer will not acknowledge to you, or maybe even to him/herself, that your candidacy has been eliminated. If you were "the one", the other candidate would not be in the picture at this late time. Many employers will use you in this situation as a "contingency" or "backup candidate," capable but not the first choice.

It is safe to say that a recruiter can help ease the burden of the waiting game. A good recruiter will maintain open lines of communication with both the employer and the candidate, in this way easing the uncertainty that would otherwise exist.

Conclusion

I believe we will all agree that the ultimate objective of your job search is to find the right job—and there are probably several "right" jobs for you—in a reasonably short period of time. In the best of circumstances, the job search in the real world is a difficult situation. This is true whether you are currently employed or not. With proper planning and good execution, the discomfort of the search can be minimized and the likelihood of finding what you want can be enhanced significantly. A fair portion of honesty (with yourself) added to the ingredients of the search will help direct you toward the most appropriate opportunities.

All of what is discussed here will not apply to everyone. For example, if you are currently employed and seeking to make a job change, you will have far less time to commit to the search and you will probably need to conduct the search with confidentiality so that your present employer does not become aware. Still, it is safe to say that conducting a job search with this book as a guide should be substantially easier than doing without. There are a few truisms, but the impact of the bulk of the knowledge shared here will be biased by the unique aspects of each individual's given set of circumstances.

If life can be described as analogous to an amusement

park, the job search would definitely be the roller coaster. Incredible high speed excitement is interspersed with moments of supreme confidence, punctuated with gut-wrenching moments of doubt! Ups and downs coming at a pace which will tie your stomach in a knot. Just when you think you have reached the peak, an unexpected turn hurls you downward faster than you thought possible. At the end, you will find the peace you are seeking which made the whole ride worthwhile. Yet, it is that element of doubt which makes the roller coaster so alluring in the first place.

Appendix

I. THE RULES OF THE JOB SEARCH

Rule #1. Allow yourself to feel those emotions arising from a job loss.

Rule #2. Carefully plan your job search in order to minimize your period of unemployment and to ultimately find the best job for you.

Rule #3. Commit to yourself that the job search is a full time job in itself and that it is the single most important activity in your life right now.

Rule #4. Only you can make it happen. Employers are not likely to seek you out. You will find a job for only one reason—because you make it happen.

Rule #5. Having all the right tools will allow you to be more efficient and make your search easier to handle.

Rule #6. How you see yourself and how you project your self image play a significant role in determining how employers react to you in making hiring decisions.

Rule #7. Being selective in choosing companies to contact is a sign that you are exercising control.

Rule #8. Every phone call should be made with a specific objective in mind.

Rule #9. Always make your initial contact, in a cold call situation, at the top of the organization or at the highest level that may be appropriate.

Rule #10. Keep your cool, be convincing, and don't let the quirks of a hiring manager undermine your attitude.

Rule #11. Networking is, by far, the most valuable means of finding job leads.

Rule #12. Give yourself a pep talk whenever possible in order to keep yourself feeling positive and focused.

Rule #13. Never accept an offer without taking a brief time to consider the position from all viewpoints.

II. SAMPLE RESUME
Resume of: Your Name
Your Address
Your phone number (including area code)

Professional Experience:
Name of your most recent employer, the dates of your employment, your current title. Brief description of company's business.

Accomplishments
- Most important accomplishment (in brief detail)
- Second most important accomplishment i.e. promotions
- Next most important accomplishment
- Etc.

Name of your second most recent employer, dates of employment, your last title. Brief description of company's business.

Accomplishments

- Your most important accomplishment
- Etc.

Names of your previous employers, etc.

Educational Background

Highest level of education completed, or degree earned, name of school, and major or course of study.

Other relevant educational accomplishments

Military Experience (If relevant)

Other Accomplishments (only if relevant)

III. THINGS YOU CAN LEAVE OFF OF YOUR RESUME

1. Earnings history
2. How you paid for college
3. Religious affiliations
4. Political opinions
5. Names of supervisors
6. References
7. "References provided upon request." (Of course you'll provide references if requested.)
8. Your age or date of birth
9. Your marital status and/or number of children
10. Any other information that is irrelevant or could cause bias

Index

G

H

I

J

L

M

N

O

P

A Short Biography of Alan Jacobson

Looking back, I doubt that I had even the faintest idea in my childhood where my life would take me. What a long strange trip it's been.

Born in Charleston, West Virginia, I grew up in the Maryland suburbs of Washington, D.C., where I went to high school and undergraduate school. I earned a B.S. from the University of Maryland, surviving the turbulent 1960s, a time for re-thinking of values, goals, and beliefs.

After a short stint living in southern California, and a job transfer back to Maryland, I began my real career in Sales and Marketing Management in the medical device industry. Fortunately for me, my first job in the industry was with a division of Johnson & Johnson. In addition to the tremendous learning experience of my nearly six years there, I was able to take advantage of one of the key benefits the company offered its employees—the educational benefit. Yes, Johnson & Johnson paid for 100% of my MBA at Loyola College of Maryland. Tuition, books, and fees!

Since that time, I have worked for five other companies in the medical device industry, working myself up to the vice president level. I have travelled on business to numerous countries and, to date, to forty-seven of the fifty states.

In my spare time, I have taught Marketing and Management on the undergraduate level at Central Connecticut State University, I have worked with a number of firms on a consulting basis, I have conducted training classes for several corporations, have dabbled in writing, and I have developed a substantially different theory regarding the stock market.

On the personal side, I have been very happily married to my wife since 1974. We have three children of middle school and high school age. What an education it has been raising them! We live in Connecticut now, arriving here from Maryland via Texas and New Jersey. In between, I have lived briefly in Pennsylvania and Wisconsin. What an education it has been living in all those places! But, I guess everything we do educates us ...if we let it.